# DIY SCIENCE

## 30 incredible home experiments

Autumn
Publishing

# Autumn
## Publishing

Published in 2018
by Autumn Publishing
Cottage Farm
Sywell
NN6 0BJ
www.igloobooks.com

GUA009 0718
2 4 6 8 10 9 7 5 3 1
ISBN 978-1-78810-371-8

Illustrated by Teemu Juhani
Written by Marnie Willow
Additional imagery © iStock / Getty images

Designed by Chris Stanley
Edited by Helen Catt

Printed and manufactured in China

# CONTENTS

HOW TO BE A SCIENTIST · · · · · · · · · · · · · · · · · · · · · · · · · · · · · · · · · · 4

PHYSICS   BOTTLE ROCKET · · · · · · · · · · · · · · · · · · · · · · · · · · · · · · 8

SOLAR OVEN · · · · · · · · · · · · · · · · · · · · · · · · · · · · · · · · 10

MARSHMALLOW CATAPULT · · · · · · · · · · · · · · · · · · · · · 12

THE LIGHT FANTASTIC · · · · · · · · · · · · · · · · · · · · · · · · · 14

BALLOON CAR RACING · · · · · · · · · · · · · · · · · · · · · · · · 16

TOY PARACHUTE · · · · · · · · · · · · · · · · · · · · · · · · · · · · 18

FLY A KITE · · · · · · · · · · · · · · · · · · · · · · · · · · · · · · · · · 20

STATIC MAGIC · · · · · · · · · · · · · · · · · · · · · · · · · · · · · · 22

SPOOKY LEMON LIGHT-UP MASK · · · · · · · · · · · · · · · · 24

BIOLOGY   SWEEPING FOR CREEPIES · · · · · · · · · · · · · · · · · · · · · 28

JUNGLE IN A JAR · · · · · · · · · · · · · · · · · · · · · · · · · · · · 30

HÔTEL DES BUGS · · · · · · · · · · · · · · · · · · · · · · · · · · · · 32

CATERPILLAR NURSERY · · · · · · · · · · · · · · · · · · · · · · · 34

BEASTLY YEAST · · · · · · · · · · · · · · · · · · · · · · · · · · · · · 36

LIVING CAKE · · · · · · · · · · · · · · · · · · · · · · · · · · · · · · · 38

MAGIC BEANS · · · · · · · · · · · · · · · · · · · · · · · · · · · · · · 40

BUILD A WORMERY · · · · · · · · · · · · · · · · · · · · · · · · · · · 42

CHEMISTRY   RED CABBAGE BLUE CABBAGE · · · · · · · · · · · · · · · · · 46

GIANT BUBBLES · · · · · · · · · · · · · · · · · · · · · · · · · · · · · 48

VOLCANO MANIA · · · · · · · · · · · · · · · · · · · · · · · · · · · · 50

INVISIBLE INK · · · · · · · · · · · · · · · · · · · · · · · · · · · · · · 52

LAVA LAMP · · · · · · · · · · · · · · · · · · · · · · · · · · · · · · · · 53

SUGAR CRYSTALS · · · · · · · · · · · · · · · · · · · · · · · · · · · · 54

PING PONG GEODES · · · · · · · · · · · · · · · · · · · · · · · · · · 56

UNICORN POOP SLIME · · · · · · · · · · · · · · · · · · · · · · · · 58

GLOW-IN-THE-DARK SUPER SLIMEY SLIME · · · · · · · · · 60

GUMMY GOO · · · · · · · · · · · · · · · · · · · · · · · · · · · · · · · 62

SLIME OLYMPICS · · · · · · · · · · · · · · · · · · · · · · · · · · · · · 64

# HOW TO BE A SCIENTIST

It's helpful to have a notebook or journal where you can write down
your notes and thoughts about the world and your experiments.

## OBSERVE

Take your science notebook out with you and take notes on things that you see. If you
go on a nature walk, write down or draw different birds, bugs or animals you spot. Keep
an eye out for fossils in rocks, or look for shooting stars in the sky. The more you notice
about the world around you, the more you'll be able to think of new questions.

## ASK QUESTIONS

Why are bubbles round? What makes rockets fly? Keep thinking of questions and writing
them down. If you find out the answer later, you can always add that to your notebook, too!

## TRY TO GUESS WHAT WILL HAPPEN (BEFORE IT HAPPENS)

This is called making a prediction. What will happen if you try to use a square hole
to blow a square bubble? What will happen if you change the shape of the rocket?
Write down what you think will happen before you do the experiment.

## DO THE EXPERIMENT

Make notes on how you do the experiment. All sorts of things can make a difference to how the results turn out. Is it hot or cold that day? Wet or dry? Did you change the experiment in any way? Then write down what happened. If you took any measurements, write them down. Draw pictures or take photos to tape into your notebook.

## COME UP WITH NEW QUESTIONS

Use the results to think up other questions. How would you do things differently next time? What do you think would change? Start the process all over again!

This process is known as the **scientific method**. People have been following these steps for over a thousand years, and it has helped scientists work out the answers to questions from "What happens if I hit this thing with a big rock?" to "What shape is the Universe?"

# NOTES FOR GROWN-UPS

Science is a big topic, so don't worry if you don't know all the answers! If your child asks you something you're not sure about, think together about how you can change the experiment to find out, or where you can look it up.

When doing these experiments with your child, keep things light and fun and let your child take the lead. Help them with the tricky bits, ask lots of questions and make sure they stay safe.

 **WARNING**

Some of the experiments in this book involve potential hazards such as heat or sharp implements. The publisher strongly recommends that parents and guardians supervise their children during ALL activities, giving particular attention to stages marked with a triangle warning sign.

Whenever starting out on one of these experiments, always read through the instructions and consider what safety precautions are necessary. It is a good idea to involve your child with this discussion: identifying risks and taking sensible precautions is a key part of laboratory life. Talk about questions like whether it would be best to wear protective clothing such as goggles or rubber gloves, and whether it is best to do the experiment inside or outside in a safe place. Always use your judgement and stay safe.

# PHYSICS

# PHYSICS

Physics is all about forces, energy and things that go whizz! Forces push and pull objects. They're what make things move fast or slowly. Energy is stuff like heat, light, movement and electricity.

Investigate some of the forces you can see in action every day, like gravity, air-resistance, friction and more, by building a whooshy rocket, an awesome parachute and a whizzy balloon car. Then discover a delicious use for heat energy from the sun and find out how you can get light from a lemon. You'll only sometimes make a mess...

# BOTTLE ROCKET

Be prepared! This whooshy, splooshy rocket makes a mess. Get ready to get drenched (and make sure you tell your parents it's all in the name of science).

## WARNING

This bottle launches **suddenly** at **high speed** and can travel long distances. Only fire it in a **wide open space** away from people and animals.

## YOU WILL NEED

- empty plastic fizzy drink bottle
- stiff card
- sticky tape
- bottle cork
- bicycle pump with needle attachment
- safety scissors

## STEP 1

Ask an adult to help push the needle of a bicycle pump through a cork. They may have to drill a hole through it first. The cork needs to fit snugly into the bottle.

## STEP 2

To make a nose cone, draw a circle on the card that is about twice as wide as the base of your bottle. Cut out the circle, then cut a slit to its centre. Curve it into a cone that fits snugly over the bottom of the bottle, then tape it in place.

## STEP 3

Cut three triangles out of card to make fins for your rocket. Use sticky tape to attach them to the bottom of the rocket, sticking out so the rocket can stand up on end.

## STEP 4

Fill the bottle so it's about a third full of water. Plug it with the cork so the needle pokes into the bottle.

## STEP 5

Stand your rocket upright, then use the pump to force air into it until it launches!

# HOW DOES IT WORK?

Forcing air into the bottle increases the pressure (push) of the air against the water. When the pressure gets too high, the air suddenly pushes the cork out of the bottle. The water sprays downwards, which pushes the rocket upwards. This is how real rockets work, except they blast out burning hot gas instead of high-pressure water!

## WHAT NEXT?

What do you think happens if you use more water? What happens if you use a bigger or smaller bottle?

# SOLAR OVEN

Create deliciously sticky snacks by melting chocolate and marshmallow together using only the awesome power of the sun.

## YOU WILL NEED

- empty cereal box
- black card
- aluminium foil
- sharp scissors
- plastic food wrap
- sticky tape
- glue
- stick
- ruler
- snack to cook!

## ⚠ WARNING

This oven can get hot enough to burn you. Ask an adult to help you and use oven gloves when handling anything hot. Do not leave unattended. Follow normal food safety rules and do not use the oven to cook raw meat or anything else that carries a risk of food poisoning.

## STEP 1

Make sure your box is clean and take out any paper or plastic liners. Then use a ruler to draw a rectangle on the large side of your box, around 3 cm from each edge.

## STEP 2

Use scissors to cut out three sides of the rectangle, leaving one side attached to form a hinge. Fold back the rectangle so it opens outwards from the box.

## STEP 3

Cover the whole of the inside of the box (including the underside of the flap) with aluminium foil. Make sure the shiny side of the foil is showing.

## STEP 4

Place a piece of black card on the bottom of the box. Place your snack on top of the black card.

## STEP 5

Use a stick to prop up the lid so it stands up straight. Completely cover the opening with plastic wrap, fixing it in place with sticky tape.

# HOW DOES IT WORK?

The oven captures heat energy from the sun. The shiny foil reflects sunlight into the oven. while the plastic wrap helps keep heat inside. Hot air rises, so without the plastic wrap, a lot of hot air would just float away. Instead this air is trapped inside the oven, getting hotter and hotter. This is how greenhouses work!

## STEP 6

⚠ Place the solar oven so it faces the sun on a hot day and wait for your snack to melt.

## WHAT NEXT?

Can you change the design of the oven to make it work better? Measure how hot it gets by using a thermometer.

## ⚠ STEP 7

When it's ready, ask an adult to carefully peel back the plastic wrap to take out the snack!

# MARSHMALLOW CATAPULT

You can't attack any castles with this catapult, but you can demonstrate the amazing conversion of potential energy into kinetic energy. If that doesn't impress your teacher, nothing will.

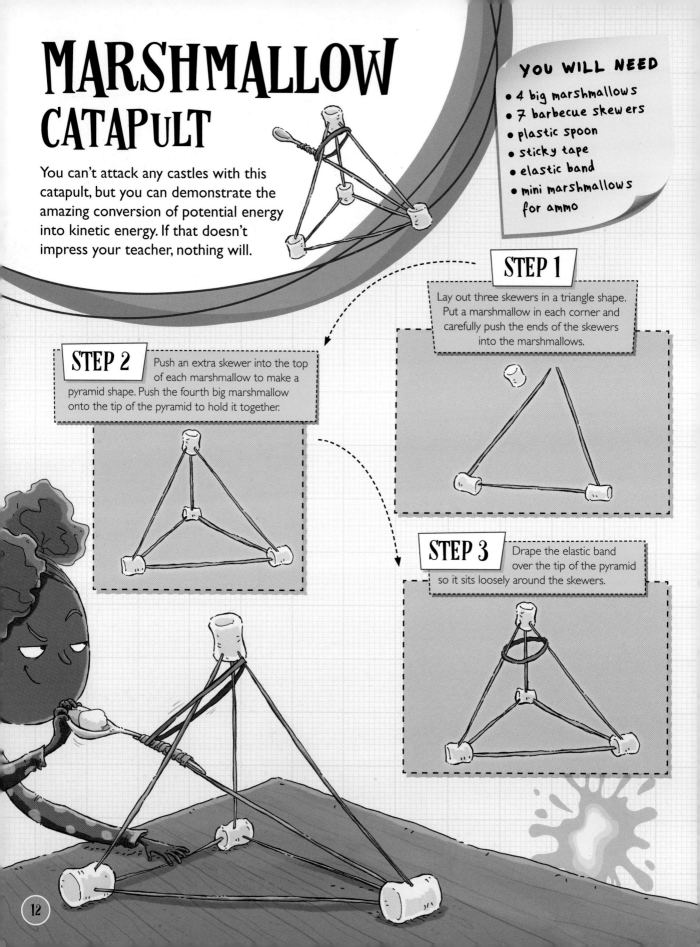

## YOU WILL NEED

- 4 big marshmallows
- 7 barbecue skewers
- plastic spoon
- sticky tape
- elastic band
- mini marshmallows for ammo

## STEP 1

Lay out three skewers in a triangle shape. Put a marshmallow in each corner and carefully push the ends of the skewers into the marshmallows.

## STEP 2

Push an extra skewer into the top of each marshmallow to make a pyramid shape. Push the fourth big marshmallow onto the tip of the pyramid to hold it together.

## STEP 3

Drape the elastic band over the tip of the pyramid so it sits loosely around the skewers.

## STEP 4

Use sticky tape to attach the plastic spoon to the top of the last skewer.

**Top tip!**
Your catapult will be stronger if you leave the marshmallows out overnight before you build it.

## STEP 5

Feed the last skewer through the elastic band and into the marshmallow in the furthest bottom corner. The skewer should rest on the elastic band.

# HOW DOES IT WORK?

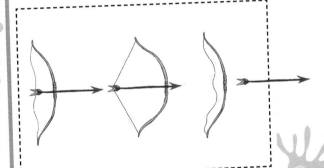

Stretching the elastic band gives it potential energy (a type of energy that has the potential to turn into other types of energy, like heat, light or movement). When you release the elastic band, the potential energy turns into movement (also called kinetic energy), launching the marshmallow across the room.

## STEP 6

Put a mini marshmallow into the spoon. Push the spoon downwards so it stretches the elastic band, and release!

## WHAT NEXT?

Draw a target on paper and see how accurately you can hit it.
Can you think of any ways to change the catapult so you can fire the marshmallows faster and further?

# THE LIGHT FANTASTIC

What colour is white light? That may sound like a trick question, but you can find out with this colourful experiment. Scatter light to make your very own indoor rainbow. Pot of gold not included.

⚠️ **WARNING**
When using the torch, avoid looking directly into the light. Ensure the light is switched off before preparation. Do not look directly into the light beam.

**Top tip!**
The darker the room is, the easier it will be to see your rainbow.

## STEP 1

Pour the water into the glass. Place the mirror under the surface of the water. Lean it against the side of the glass so it stands on its edge.

## STEP 2

Use black sticky tape to cover most of the torch's head, so only a thin strip of light can get through.

## STEP 3

Shine the torch through the glass at the mirror and look for your rainbow!

# HOW DOES IT WORK?

White light is made up of lots of colours. When a ray of light moves between air and water, it bends (refracts). Violet light bends more than red light, so the colours split up and spread out. When the colours reflect (bounce) off the mirror, they spread out even more.

This is how rainbows form in the sky. Millions of tiny water droplets act like the glass and the mirror to refract and reflect sunlight, scattering the colours to make a rainbow.

Prove light is made up of different colours! Take a paper plate and split it into seven sections. Colour the sections in the colours of the rainbow: red, orange, yellow, green, blue, indigo and violet. Push a pencil through the middle of the plate, then spin it like a top. What do you notice?

## WHAT NEXT?

Try another mini experiment to see refraction in action. Draw a horizontal arrow on a piece of card and look at it through the glass of water. Slowly move the card backwards away from the glass. What do you notice?

# BALLOON CAR RACING

In this whizzy experiment, you can demonstrate Newton's third law of motion: every action has an equal and opposite reaction. This is just a fancy way of saying if you push your little brother, he pushes back just as hard.

## YOU WILL NEED

- cardboard
- scissors
- 2 barbecue skewers
- sticky tack
- balloon
- 2 straight straws
- 1 bendy straw
- sticky tape
- 4 fast food drinks lids

## STEP 1

Cut a rectangle of cardboard to make the base of your car. It should be slightly narrower than the barbecue skewers.

## STEP 2

To make the axles, trim the straight straws so they're 2 cm shorter than the skewers. Thread a skewer through the middle of each straw. Push the drinks lids onto the ends of the skewers and secure them with balls of sticky tack.

## STEP 3

Attach the axles to the base of your car with sticky tape. Make sure the skewers can still move freely inside the straws.

## STEP 4

Feed the top of the bendy straw into the balloon. Use sticky tape to create an airtight seal between the balloon and the straw. Attach the straw to the top of the car's base with sticky tape, so the end of the straw sticks out a bit.

## STEP 5

Blow up the balloon. Place the car in starter's position and release!

# HOW DOES IT WORK?

When you blow up the balloon, you stretch the elastic by filling it with air at a high pressure. When you release the balloon, the elastic pushes the air back out. The air whooshes backwards, pushing the car forwards.

# WHAT NEXT?

Try making different designs for your race cars. Then set up a racetrack and see which design is fastest. Use a stopwatch to measure their times.

# TOY PARACHUTE

Is it a bird? Is it a plane? No, it's Pilot Ted making an emergency crash landing. Luckily, with a plastic bag and a yogurt pot, you can make his landing soft as a cloud.

## YOU WILL NEED

- large plastic bag
- scissors
- sticky tack
- sharp pencil
- marker pen
- thread or fishing line
- sticky tape
- empty yogurt pot
- ruler

## STEP 1

Cut along the side and bottom of the plastic bag. Open it up to make a large, flat sheet.

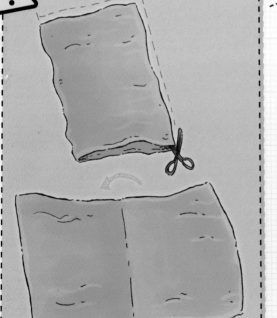

## STEP 2

Use the thread to tie the pencil and the marker pen together, 20 cm apart. Pierce the plastic sheet with the pencil and use sticky tack to hold it in place. Keep the thread taut to draw a circle with the marker. Carefully cut out the circle.

## STEP 3

Measure eight pieces of thread 30 cm long. Pierce eight holes around the edge of the circle. Tie a piece of thread through each hole. Use sticky tape to secure and strengthen the places where the string joins.

# HOW DOES IT WORK?

slow fall

fast plummet

Objects accelerate (speed up) when the forces pulling or pushing in one direction are stronger than the forces pulling or pushing in the other direction. When you drop Pilot Ted, gravity pulls him down towards the ground, while air resistance pushes up against him. A parachute increases the area that the air pushes against. This increases the force of the air resistance and stops Ted speeding up as much, giving him a gentle landing.

## STEP 4

Pierce four holes in your yogurt pot. Into each hole, tie two of the threads from the parachute. The pot should hang like a hot-air balloon basket.

## STEP 5

Put your toy in the yogurt pot. Take the parachute to a high, safe place and drop!

## WHAT NEXT?

Try making parachutes in different shapes and sizes. Which works best? Can you make a parachute that works well enough that you can drop an egg without it cracking?

# FLY A KITE

How does something fly when it's heavier than air? It's all down to a force called lift. Helicopters, aeroplanes and kites all rely on it to fly. Make a kite to investigate.

## WARNING

Only fly your kite in open spaces away from moving objects and cars, trees and overhead power lines. Do not use in high winds, or allow the string to be drawn through your hands at speed. Release slowly, keeping the line tight.

## YOU WILL NEED

- stiff wrapping paper
- 2 long, thin wooden (dowling) rods
- thin string
- scissors
- ribbons
- sticky tape

## STEP 1

Ask an adult to saw the wooden rods so one is 90 cm long and the other is 50 cm long. Ask them to saw grooves or slits into the flat edges at the ends of the rods.

## STEP 2

Cross the wooden rods over each other and tie tightly in place, making an 'X' shape with the string.

## STEP 3

Tie string around the bottom of the frame, leaving 30 cm loose. Pull the string taut around the frame, feeding it through the slits on the ends of the rods. Tie the string tightly at the bottom, leaving another 30 cm free.

## STEP 4

Cut a piece of string 50 cm long. Tie it either end of the short rod. You can wrap some sticky tape over the knot to keep it in place.

## STEP 5 ⚠️

Place the kite frame on the wrapping paper. Draw around the string outline, adding about 2 cm extra all the way around. Cut out your kite shape, making sure you don't cut the loose strings.

## STEP 6

Glue or tape the frame in place on the paper. Fold the paper over the string, using sticky tape to hold it in place.

## STEP 7

Take the string that you tied across the horizontal bar of the kite frame. Loop the end of the ball of string around its middle and tie tightly.

## STEP 8

Tie the ribbons to the strings at the bottom of the kite to make a tail. Take your kite to a safe place outside to fly it!

# HOW DOES IT WORK?

The shape of the kite means most of the wind moves underneath it, pushing the kite upwards. This push is the force called lift. The pull of the string downwards is equal to the push of the lift upwards, so the forces are balanced and the kite stays in the same place. The kite's tail also pulls downwards, so the kite stays steady and doesn't spin.

# WHAT NEXT?
Does running with the kite help it fly? What happens if you change the length of the kite's tail? What happens if you try to fly the kite with no tail at all?

21

# STATIC MAGIC

You can see static in action in a thunder storm. Negative electrical charge builds up in the clouds until it zaps down to the ground as lightning. This is a huge-scale version of what happens when you scuff your feet on carpet, then touch someone and give them an electric shock. Zap!

## YOU WILL NEED

- lametta tinsel
- PVC pipe
- wool or silk cloth
- polystyrene plates
- tissue paper
- balloons

### STEP 1

Use very thin lametta tinsel (about 1.5 mm across works best). Tie 6 strands together at the end. Measure 15 cm along, then tie a second knot, trimming the ends.

### STEP 2

Take a piece of PVC pipe and rub it with a cloth to give it charge.

### STEP 3

Hold the tinsel ball above the pipe, but don't let them touch! Gently wave the pipe to make the ball hover.

## HOVER PLATE

Rub two polystyrene plates with a cloth to give them static charge. Turn one polystyrene plate upside down and try to place the other plate on top. Can you make it hover?

## BEND WATER

Charge a balloon by rubbing it against your hair. Turn on a tap so that a thin, steady stream of water comes out. Bring the balloon close to the water (but don't let it touch). Can you make the water bend?

## HOW DOES IT WORK?

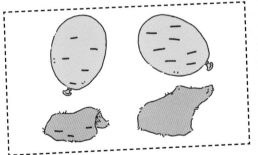

Static is an electrical charge that can build up on an object. This charge can be positive or negative. Balloons can pick up negative charge when you rub them with a wool or silk cloth. Objects with opposite charges, like the paper and the balloon, are attracted to each other, while objects with the same charge, like the tinsel ball and the PVC pipe, are repelled (pushed away) from each other.

## PAPER PIECES

Cut out tiny pieces of tissue paper. Charge a balloon by rubbing it against your hair or a cloth. Hold the balloon above the tissue paper. What happens?

# SPOOKY LEMON LIGHT-UP MASK

Terrify your friends and family with this spooky lemon light-up mask. Choose a dark and stormy night for this experiment to give it extra scare factor.

## YOU WILL NEED

- 2 lemons
- 2 copper pennies
- 2 small galvanised (zinc) nails
- sharp knife
- 2 small LED bulbs
- 4 wires with crocodile clips
- cardboard

## STEP 1

Draw a spooky mask on a piece of cardboard. Ask an adult to cut it out, making sure they cut a couple of small holes for the eyes, just large enough for the LED lights to slot through.

## STEP 2

Ask an adult to use the knife to cut two slits through the rind on opposite ends of the lemon.

## STEP 3

Put the penny through one of the slits and the nail through the other slit. Make sure the two objects don't touch inside the lemon.

## STEP 4

Connect the crocodile clip at the end of one of the wires to the penny. Then connect the other wire to the nail.

# HOW DOES IT WORK?

Batteries are made by putting different kinds of metal into an acid. A chemical reaction between the acid and the metals generates electricity. In your circuit, the acid in the lemon juice reacts with the coin and the nail to turn your lemon into a battery. The wires and the bulb complete the circuit and the bulb lights up.

## STEP 5

Connect the free ends of both wires to the connectors on the bulb.

## STEP 6

Repeat steps 2–5 to make a second circuit, then slot the two glowing lights into the mask. Hide it somewhere spooky and wait for it to give someone a scare!

# BIOLOGY

# BIOLOGY

Biology is the study of living things. That includes plants and animals (including humans), as well as other living things like yeast and mould.

Lots of biology involves studying living things in their natural habitat, so you'll definitely get muddy doing a lot of these experiments. See what kind of bugs live near you in a park or your garden, then build a bug hotel to encourage new ones to visit. You'll also discover which common garden visitor might one day help humans live on Mars.

# SWEEPING FOR CREEPIES

How many creepy crawlies are lurking in the long grass? With a swish of your sweep net, you can discover the tiny world of minibeasts. Just make sure you put all bugs back where you found them!

**YOU WILL NEED**
- wire coat hanger
- garden cane
- old white pillowcase
- strong sticky tape
- shoebox

## STEP 1

Stretch out the loop of the coat hanger to make a circle.

## ⚠ STEP 2

Straighten out the hook of the coat hanger, then carefully wrap it around the garden cane. Use strong tape to stick it in place, making sure to cover the sharp end of the hanger.

## STEP 3

Fold the edge of the pillowcase over the circle loop and tape it in place.

## STEP 4

Sweep the net slowly through long grass. Then carefully turn out the net into your shoebox to see what you've found.

# WHAT NEXT?

Draw or photograph the minibeasts you've found. Do any of them look like the ones below? Try looking in the same bit of grass in different weather conditions or at different times through the year. Do you find different bugs?

**Ants** live in vast groups or colonies with millions of other ants. They work together to feed the colony, so if you see one, there are probably more close by...

**Beetles** are insects with hard shells or exoskeletons. Their shells act like hard armour to protect the beetles from predators.

**Caterpillars** munch on leaves until they're big enough to form a pupa and turn into a butterfly.

Watch out for hairy caterpillars! Some of them can give you a nasty rash.

**Centipedes and millipedes** often hide in leaf mulch and in other shadowy places, but you might spot a few in your net.

**Crickets and grasshoppers** have strong back legs that let them leap ten times their body length, so watch out!

**Spiders** have eight legs and spin sticky webs that trap other insects so the spiders can eat them.

**Slugs and snails** like to munch on fresh leaves, so you may spot some in the long grass, especially if it's been raining.

29

# JUNGLE IN A JAR

Terrariums are mini habitats where you control the surroundings to suit your plants. Ferns have been around for millions of years, so they're perfect for creating a Jurassic jungle home for any pet dinosaurs you may have.

**Top tip!**
You can buy activated charcoal from garden centres or pet shops.

## STEP 1

Pour a layer of gravel into the bottom of the jar, then sprinkle a thin layer of activated charcoal on top of the gravel.

## STEP 2

Cover the charcoal with a layer of compost at least 5 cm thick.

## STEP 3

Use a small trowel or old wooden spoon to dig a hole in the compost. Gently place your first plant in the hole. Cover the roots with compost and press down lightly to firm it in.

## STEP 4

Continue to dig in the plants and moss, arranging them however you want. Add the lichen-covered twigs. If you like, you can decorate your terrarium by adding rocks, pebbles or plastic toys!

## MINI RAINFOREST

Make a rainforest terrarium using tiny bromeliads and polkadot plants, as well as the ferns and mosses. Keep the terrarium warm in indirect sunlight.

## MINI DESERT

Build a desert terrarium using succulents and cacti (be careful handling the cacti). Keep lots of space between the different plants, use a container with a large opening and keep it in a warm, light, airy place.

## TERRARIUM CARE

Keep your terrarium moist, not wet. Spray it with water occasionally. Snip off any dead leaves with scissors and take them out of the terrarium to keep the plants healthy.

# HÔTEL DES BUGS

Give your mini garden visitors a stay to remember with this deluxe bug hotel, filled with only the finest pinecones and rotting wood. It might not be your parents' idea of luxury, but the bugs will love it!

## STEP 1

Choose a cool, damp place for your bug hotel. Make sure the ground is firm and fairly flat. Make two sides of a rectangle using eight bricks, four on either side.

## STEP 2

Fill the space between the bricks with old logs and straw. Loosely place the tiles on top.

## STEP 3

Stack another set of eight bricks on top of the first eight bricks. Fill the space with more garden stuff. Make sure you create lots of nooks and crannies for different creatures to hide in.

## STEP 4

Keep adding layers of bricks and garden stuff, using different stuff to fill each layer. When you're done, finish it off with the roofing felt to keep the rain off the insides.

# WHAT NEXT?

Keep checking your bug hotel over several weeks to see what critters have moved in. Different bugs like different conditions. Does your hotel attract any of the beasties below?

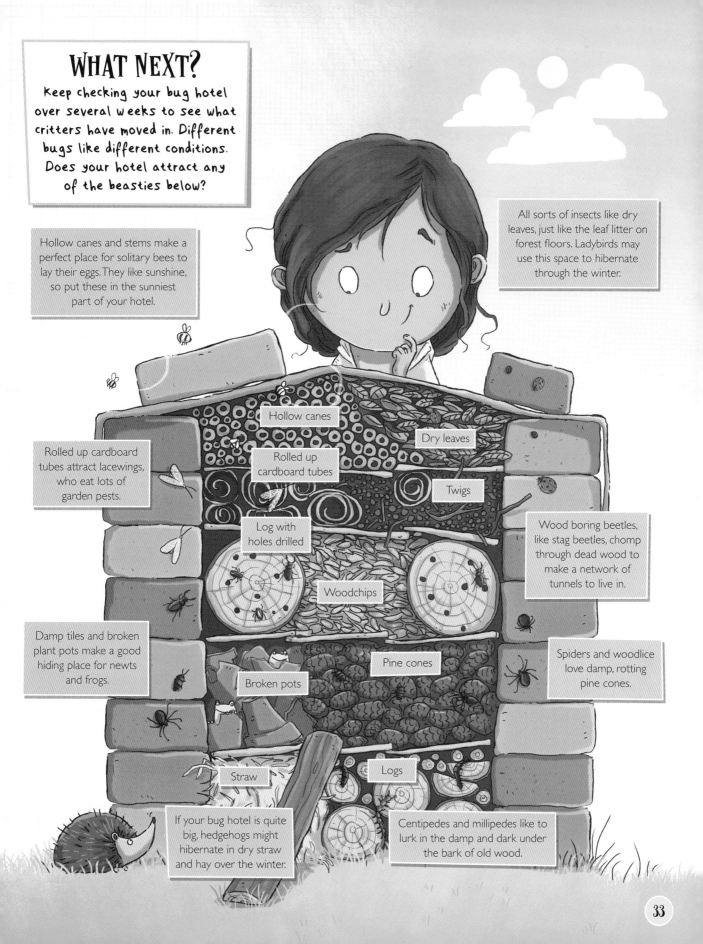

All sorts of insects like dry leaves, just like the leaf litter on forest floors. Ladybirds may use this space to hibernate through the winter.

Hollow canes and stems make a perfect place for solitary bees to lay their eggs. They like sunshine, so put these in the sunniest part of your hotel.

Rolled up cardboard tubes attract lacewings, who eat lots of garden pests.

Damp tiles and broken plant pots make a good hiding place for newts and frogs.

Wood boring beetles, like stag beetles, chomp through dead wood to make a network of tunnels to live in.

Spiders and woodlice love damp, rotting pine cones.

If your bug hotel is quite big, hedgehogs might hibernate in dry straw and hay over the winter.

Centipedes and millipedes like to lurk in the damp and dark under the bark of old wood.

Hollow canes

Dry leaves

Rolled up cardboard tubes

Twigs

Log with holes drilled

Woodchips

Pine cones

Broken pots

Straw

Logs

# CATERPILLAR NURSERY

Children. They grow up so fast. Only yesterday, you could hear the pitter-patter of dozens of tiny feet and now here they are, ready to fly away and lay their own eggs. Wait, not children. Caterpillars.

## YOU WILL NEED

- large plastic tub
- kitchen paper
- thin tea towel
- caterpillar volunteers
- leaves
- twigs
- paintbrush
- water spray bottle

## ⚠ WARNING

Look online to identify the caterpillars before you take them away from the plant. Don't take any caterpillars that are rare or that could cause skin irritation if touched.

**Top tip!**
Caterpillars are fussy eaters. Only feed them leaves from the plant you found them on.

### STEP 1

Ask an adult to cut a large hole in the lid of the plastic tub. Leave the outside of the lid intact.

### STEP 2

Line the tub with kitchen paper and spray lightly with water to make it damp. Add leaves and twigs from the same plant where you found the caterpillars.

### STEP 3

Hold the paintbrush over the caterpillars and let them crawl on, one at a time. Carefully lift the caterpillars into the plastic tub.

### STEP 4

Lay the tea towel over the top of the tub, then firmly press on the lid on top.

# HOW DOES IT WORK?

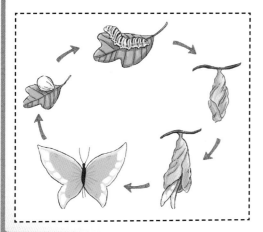

By the time you've found your caterpillar volunteers, they've already hatched from their tiny eggs. Their one job after that is to eat. The more they eat, the faster they grow. When they're big enough, they find a safe place and become a pupa. Inside the hard, protective pupa, their bodies turn into soupy goo that rearranges itself into a butterfly's body shape. When their bodies have completely rebuilt themselves, the pupa peels open and the butterflies emerge, ready to live fulfilling butterfly lives.

## CATERPILLAR CARE

1. Make sure the caterpillars have fresh leaves to eat every day. Swap the old kitchen paper for new every few days.

2. Don't panic if you find caterpillar skins around the box. Caterpillars shed their skin as they grow bigger.

3. When the caterpillars change into pupae, make sure you don't disturb them.

4. When the butterflies emerge, they will need time to let their wings harden before they can fly.

5. When the butterflies are ready, release them outside on a warm, sunny day.

# BEASTLY YEAST

Yeast is part of the fungus kingdom, along with moulds and mushrooms. In this case, a kingdom is one of the five groups of living things (fungi, plants, animals, bacteria and protists), not a place ruled by the mushroom king.

## ⚠ WARNING

Warning! Children under eight years can choke or suffocate on uninflated or broken balloons. Adult supervision required. Keep uninflated balloons from children. Discard broken balloons at once.

**STEP 1** Label your three bottles "hot", "warm" and "cold".

**STEP 2** Ask an adult to mix cold and hot water until they have 200 ml of water that is about 50 °C. Pour this water into the bottle marked "hot".

**STEP 3** Next add 200 ml of warm water (you should be able to comfortably hold your hand in it) to the bottle labelled "warm". Then pour 200 ml of iced water into the bottle marked "cold".

**STEP 4** Add 3 spoonfuls of sugar and a spoonful of yeast to each bottle. Swill the bottles gently to help mix in the sugar.

## STEP 5

Put the balloons over the tops of the bottles and see what happens.

Yeast breaks down sugar to get energy that lets it grow and make new yeast cells. This reaction gives off gas (carbon dioxide), which bubbles up and fills the balloon. The warmer the environment, the faster yeast breaks down sugar and the more gas is given off. However, once it gets hotter than body temperature, the yeast cells start to be destroyed and the reaction slows down to a halt.

## WHAT NEXT?

Try feeding your yeast different amounts of sugar. Does it make a difference to how quickly the balloons blow up?

# LIVING CAKE

Put everything you learned about yeast into practice with this living cake mix. This cake needs looking after, feeding and keeping warm for a few days. Think of it as your oozy, gooey new pet.

### To Start
- 150 g plain flour
- 225 g caster sugar
- 1 packet dried yeast
- 250 ml warm milk
- 50 ml water

## ⚠ WARNING
Ask an adult to handle hot things (including the oven), using oven gloves to avoid burns. Follow normal food safety rules.

## SCHEDULE

Look after your cake by following these instructions for nine days. Make sure you observe and make notes on how your cake looks and what changes day by day. Is it bubbly? Is it growing bigger?

**DAY 1** Mix the cake well.

**DAY 2** Mix the cake well.

**DAY 3** The yeast in your cake mix needs feeding. Add 100 g flour, 100 g sugar and 200 ml milk.

**DAY 4** Mix the cake well.

**DAY 5** Mix the cake well.

**DAY 6** Mix the cake well.

**DAY 7** The yeast in your cake mix needs feeding again! Add another 100 g flour, 100 g sugar and 200 ml milk.

**DAY 8** Mix the cake well.

**DAY 9** Your cake should now be ready to bake. Split the mix into four equal portions. Give three to your friends along with a copy of this schedule so they can make their own living cake. Then take the fourth portion and follow the instructions on the next page to bake.

## STEP 1
Mix the yeast with the warm water. Leave for 10 minutes, then stir.

## STEP 2
Add the flour and sugar, then mix thoroughly. Stir the milk in slowly.

## STEP 3
Find a safe home for your cake to live while it grows. It must be somewhere warm and dry where it can be safely left without a lid (cover it loosely with a tea towel). Do not keep it in the fridge!

## To Bake

- 225 g sugar
- 300 g plain flour
- 160 ml vegetable oil
- 2 eggs
- 1 tsp vanilla essence
- 2 grated cooking apples
- 100 g walnuts
- 2 tsp cinnamon
- 2 tsp baking powder
- 50 g melted butter
- A sprinkling of brown sugar
- 23 cm cake tin

**STEP 4** Mix all of your ingredients (except the butter and brown sugar) into a quarter of the living cake mix.

**STEP 5** Pour the whole mix into a cake tin, then pour the melted butter over it and sprinkle on the brown sugar.

**STEP 6** Bake the cake at 180 °C (350 °F) for 45 minutes, or until the top is golden brown and springs back when pressed lightly – ask an adult to help.

### Top tip!
You can experiment with lots of different flavours for your cake. Try pear, chocolate chips, cherries, almonds, raisins or anything else you like!

# MAGIC BEANS

To make a seed germinate and begin to grow, you need **WOW**! That's **W**ater, **O**xygen (air) and **W**armth. Now wow your friends and family with your super science knowledge.

**Top tip!**
Soak the beans for 24 hours first to kickstart germination.

**STEP 1** Cut a piece of blotting paper the same height as your jar.

**STEP 2** Roll the paper into a cylinder and slide it into the jam jar.

The water makes the hard outer casing of the bean swell up and split. A tiny root grows from the gap.

The root grows downwards and a tiny shoot emerges. They use energy stored inside the seed to grow.

## STEP 3

Push a bean between the paper and the side of the jar. Add a little bit of water to the bottom of the jar.

## WHAT NEXT?

Take photographs or draw the beans in your record book. Label the different parts and make notes on what you see. Try keeping different jars in different conditions (dark or light, moist or dry, warm or cold, etc.) and recording how fast each one grows.

## STEP 4

Put the jar on a warm, sunny windowsill and check on it every day to see what has changed.

The plant grows more quickly. Soon, it uses up all of the energy stored inside the seed and instead starts using the energy from sunlight to make its own food in its leaves.

The shoot grows upwards, making the plant's stem. Both the shoot and the root start to branch out. Lots of little, thread-like rootlets make a large surface area for the plant to take up water.

41

# BUILD A WORMERY

Worms are the wriggly cornerstones of entire ecosystems. After studying them for nearly 40 years, Charles Darwin (a famous old scientist) said that life couldn't exist on earth without them. Build a wormery to see why!

## YOU WILL NEED
- jar with a lid
- sand
- soil
- dead leaves
- worm food
- sticky tape
- worm volunteers
- trowel

**STEP 1** Put a thin layer of sand inside the jar. Add a layer of soil on top of the sand. Switch between layers of sand and soil until the jar is about half full.

**STEP 2** Add worm food. Dead leaves, vegetable peelings, overripe fruit and used tea leaves all work well.

## STEP 3

Now for the mucky bit. Use a trowel to carefully dig for worms in a muddy bit of the garden. This works best after the rain. Carefully place the worms on top of the worm food in the jar.

## STEP 4

Ask an adult to poke holes in the jar lid. Leave the jar in a cool, dark place for a few weeks, checking on the worms every few days. Make sure the soil stays damp but not wet.

## HOW DOES IT WORK?

Worms are detritovores, which means they eat rubbish like dead leaves and old fruit. As they wriggle underground, they mix trails of broken down plants with the soil. New plants can then take up nutrients (food) from these trails through their roots. Scientists are experimenting to see if earthworms can help make the soil on Mars suitable for growing plants. In future, worms may be the key to humans living on Mars!

## WHAT NEXT?

Test how good your worm compost is. Plant two seedlings in pots, using plain soil for one and using your worm compost for the other (let the worms go first!). Which grows biggest?

# CHEMISTRY

# CHEMISTRY

Everything is made out of chemicals. Even you're made out of chemicals. Chemistry is the science of how all those different chemicals behave and how they react with each other. Sometimes those reactions can be pretty explosive!

Find out why slime is slimey, and how crystals grow and how to make a VERY messy volcano erupt. Is chemistry the squelchiest, gooiest, most explosive type of science there is? Maybe. You'll have to try the experiments to know for sure.

# RED CABBAGE BLUE CABBAGE

Ahhh, the sweet, cabbage-y smell of science. Amaze your family with this colour-changing magic potion. You don't need to tell them that the magic is actually science!

> ⚠ **WARNING**
> Take care handling sharp knives and boiling water. Avoid strong acids and alkilis as they can be **corrosive** and **dangerous.**

## STEP 1
Ask an adult to help finely chop the red cabbage.

## STEP 2
Put the chopped cabbage in the bowl, then ask an adult to pour boiling water to cover the cabbage. Leave the cabbage mix for 15 minutes.

## STEP 3
Bash the cabbage with a wooden spoon to release more of the purple colour.

## STEP 4
Strain the cabbage through a sieve, catching the purple water in a jug.

## STEP 5

Take three clear glasses of water. Leave one as pure water. Squeeze some lemon juice into one and mix a teaspoon of baking soda into the other.

## STEP 6

Now for the weird bit. Pour a little bit of the purple cabbage potion into each glass and see the strange results.

# HOW DOES IT WORK?

Red cabbage contains a chemical called an indicator. Indicators change colour when they come into contact with things that are acidic or alkaline. Acidic liquids include lemon juice and vinegar, while alkaline liquids include soaps and water mixed with baking soda. The more drastic the colour change, the stronger the acid or alkali is.

# WHAT NEXT?

Ask an adult to help you find liquids around the house that you can test. Can you create a scale of acids and alkalis of different strengths?

# GIANT BUBBLES

Get ready to blow some epic-sized bubbles.
Prepare your bubble mix the night before
if you want your bubbles to be truly huge.

## YOU WILL NEED

- washing up liquid
- glycerin
- water
- 2 long wooden rods
- string (bakers' twine works best!)
- washer
- screw eyes (from a DIY shop)

## STEP 1

Find a large, shallow container and fill it between 5–10 cm deep with water.

## STEP 2

Add washing up liquid to the water. There should be about three times as much water as there is washing up liquid. Mix gently.

## STEP 3

Add a couple of teaspoons of glycerin. This is optional, but helps your bubbles be extra strong.

## STEP 4

To make your bubble wand, ask an adult to screw the screw eyes into the tops of the wooden rods.

## STEP 5

⚠️

Cut two lengths of string, one 50 cm and the other 1 m long. Thread the washer onto the longer string.

## STEP 6

Tie both strings to the screw eyes on the ends of the wooden rods.

## STEP 7

Hold the two wooden rods together and dip them into the bubble mix so the string is soaked through. Carefully lift the string out of the bubble mix, separating the wooden rods, and wave the wands gently.

## HOW DOES IT WORK?

Bubbles are like balloons made of soapy water instead of rubber. You can make bubbles out of plain water by blowing through a straw, but they're small and burst quickly. Adding soap changes how elastic the surface of the water is, meaning you can make bigger, longer lasting bubbles. The air inside the bubble pushes outwards, while the elastic soapy water pulls inwards (just like the rubber of a balloon). This elasticity is called surface tension, and is the reason why bubbles are round.

## WHAT NEXT?

Instead of glycerin, try adding different ingredients to the bubble mix, such as baking powder, sugar or corn syrup. Which makes the biggest or longest-lasting bubbles?

# VOLCANO MANIA

If you want to get straight to making things fizz, skip steps 1–4 and make a volcano out of dirt in the garden instead!

## ⚠ WARNING

It is recommended that you build and erupt your volcano in an outside area, easily cleaned and away from stainable or sensitive objects and plants.

## STEP 1

First build your volcano. Use the gloopy glue to stick the base of your bottle onto the cardboard.

## STEP 2

When the glue on the bottle has dried, make a mixture of $1/3$ water to $2/3$ gloopy glue. Scrunch up whole pieces of newspaper into balls, and dip them into the glue mixture. Arrange them around the base of the bottle to make a volcano shape.

## STEP 3

Tear more newspaper into thin strips. Place them over the scrunched-up newspaper, then brush glue mix over the strips. Make sure you don't cover the top of the bottle!

## STEP 4

Sprinkle sand over the volcano to make it look realistic, then wait a day for the glue to dry. Alternatively, wait for the glue to dry, then paint your volcano.

## STEP 5

Mix together 400 ml of white vinegar, 100 ml of cold water, 10 ml of dish soap and some red food colouring. Use the funnel to pour the mix into the bottle.

## STEP 6

Mix 2 tablespoons of baking soda with a little bit of water to make a liquid slurry.

## STEP 7

Pour the baking soda slurry into the bottle, and stand back!

# HOW DOES IT WORK?

Your volcano erupts when gas given off by the reaction between vinegar and baking soda reaches a high pressure, causing the liquid to fizz up and out of the volcano. Real life volcanoes work in a similar way, except the high pressure gas is superheated water vapour. This is from ocean water that has seeped through cracks in the Earth's crust into the molten-rock mantle beneath. And instead of red soapy liquid, there's red-hot lava!

# INVISIBLE INK

This science experiment can be used to send secret messages, making it perfect for top-secret spy missions or detecting clues to crack a case.

## YOU WILL NEED

- lemon
- paintbrush
- paper
- hairdryer

## STEP 1

Cut a lemon in half and squeeze out the juice into a glass.

## HOW DOES IT WORK?

The acid in the lemon juice weakens the paper where it touches it. When you heat the paper, the weaker parts burn and turn brown before the rest of the paper, revealing your secret message!

## STEP 2

Use a paintbrush to write your secret message. Don't let anyone peek!

## WHAT NEXT?

What else can you use to write your secret message? Is there a way to test other liquids to see if they would act the same way as the acidic lemon juice?

## STEP 3

Wait for your message to dry. If you want, you can write another non-secret message in pencil over the top.

## STEP 4

Reveal your message by gently heating the paper with a hairdryer or in a warm oven.

# LAVA LAMP

Make a groovy lava lamp that's just as perfect for a 70s disco as it is for showing how liquids with different densities behave. Now play that funky music, you coolcat!

## YOU WILL NEED

- vegetable oil
- water
- food colouring
- dissolvable fizzy candy
- clear bottle

## HOW DOES IT WORK?

Water and oil don't mix. Water is more dense (heavier) than oil, so it sinks underneath the oil. When the fizzy candy dissolves in the water, it gives off tiny bubbles of gas. These bubbles lift the coloured water to the surface. At the surface, the gas inside the bubbles floats away into the air, and the water sinks back down.

### STEP 1
Fill a glass three quarters full of vegetable oil, then top it up with water.

### STEP 2
Add several drops of food colouring.

### STEP 3
Break the candy into small pieces and drop one into the glass. Keep adding the rest of the pieces to keep the bubbles moving!

## WHAT NEXT?
What changes if you use warmer water? Does the experiment still work if you put the bottle cap on?

# SUGAR CRYSTALS

Grow some colourful crystals. In this experiment, you can eat the results! Who said science couldn't be delicious?

## YOU WILL NEED

- hot water
- 500 g-1.2 kg sugar
- large heatproof jug
- food colouring
- lolly pop sticks
- 4 jars
- 4 clothes pegs

## WARNING

Always ask an adult to help with handling hot water and glassware.

## STEP 2

Slowly add sugar, mixing carefully until no more sugar will dissolve. You might not need all the sugar.

## STEP 1

Ask an adult to pour 400 ml of boiling water into the heatproof jug.

## STEP 3

Add a few drops of food colouring to each of the jars.

## STEP 4

Carefully pour the sugar water into the jars. Make sure to leave any undissolved grains of sugar at the bottom of the jug.

## STEP 5
Dip the lolly pop sticks in water then roll them in sugar.

## STEP 6
Clip the unsugared ends of the lolly pop sticks to the clothes pegs. Balance the pegs on top of the jars so the sticks are suspended in the solution. Don't let the sticks touch the sides or bottoms of the jars.

## STEP 7
Cover the jars and check on them every day for three days. See how big you can grow the crystals before you take them out to eat!

# HOW DOES IT WORK?

A solution is a mix of two chemicals, like sugar dissolved in water. If you keep adding sugar to water, you'll reach a point where no more can dissolve and the mixture is saturated. But if you heat the mixture (adding heat energy), you can dissolve even more sugar, making the solution **supersaturated**. When the solution cools down, it can no longer hold the extra sugar, so sugar crystals form on the lolly sticks. Over time, water evaporates and the solution gets stronger again as there's the same amount of sugar in less water. This excess sugar crystallises and the crystals on the lolly sticks grow.

# PING PONG GEODES

Real geodes are found inside rocks and take millions of years to form. These are a bit quicker, but they're made a similar way and they're just as sparkly!

## ⚠ WARNING
Always ask an adult to help with handling hot water and glassware.

**STEP 1** Ask an adult to cut a ping pong ball in half.

**STEP 2** Use a paint brush to spread glue on the inside of the ping pong ball. Then sprinkle alum powder over the glue and leave to dry.

**STEP 3** Mix hot water with alum powder and food colouring. Add the alum power one spoonful at a time until no more will dissolve.

**STEP 4** Cool for half an hour, then use a spoon to plunge the ping pong balls under the surface of the liquid.

## STEP 5

Leave the solution overnight, then carefully lift out the geodes. Place them on a piece of kitchen roll to dry.

Natural geodes form in air pockets left after bubbly volcanic lava cools and hardens into solid rock. Over time, water trickles through the rocky ground into the air pocket, picking up minerals on the way. When this water seeps out of the air pocket, the minerals are left behind. At first, the minerals form tiny crystals, too small to see. But over millions of years, the crystals grow as more minerals are deposited on top.

## WHAT NEXT?

What happens if you leave your geodes in the alum solution for a longer time? What happens if you put the solution in the fridge overnight?

# UNICORN POOP SLIME

Unicorn poop slime is a highly scientific substance called a non-Newtonian fluid. Find out more on page 61.

Find out more on page 61.

## YOU WILL NEED

- 250 g white PVA glue (school glue)
- 2 tsp baking soda
- food colouring
- vanilla essence for smell
- big squirt of shaving foam
- contact lens solution (make sure it contains boric acid)

**STEP 1** Put your PVA glue in a large bowl and add the baking soda. Mix well (it should look a little bit fizzy).

**STEP 2** Add a few drops of food colouring and mix it until you're happy with the colour. Be careful – if you add too much food colouring, the slime might stain!

**STEP 3** Squirt in shaving foam and mix it in.

**STEP 4** Slowly add the contact lens solution, about 1 tsp at a time. Mix each tsp in thoroughly before adding the next.

**STEP 5** When the slime starts to come away from the edge of the bowl, you can use your hand to take it out of the bowl and start kneading the slime. Keep adding contact lens solution a tiny bit at a time until the slime is the perfect stretchy consistency.

**Top tip!**
If you want multicolour unicorn poop, make several batches of slime in different colours, then knead them all together at the end.

# GLOW-IN-THE-DARK SUPER SLIMEY SLIME

Is this the ooziest, gooiest, stretchiest, slimiest glow-in-the-dark slime you've ever made? There's only one way to find out.

## YOU WILL NEED

- 100 g clear PVA glue
- 50 ml water
- 1 tsp baking soda
- glycerin
- glow-in-the-dark poster paint
- contact lens solution (containing boric acid)

**STEP 1** Mix the PVA glue and water really thoroughly in a large bowl.

**STEP 2** Add the baking soda, a small squirt of poster paint and a couple of drops of glycerin. Mix thoroughly.

**STEP 3** Add the contact lens solution a little bit at a time. Make sure you've mixed in any clumps of harder slime before adding the next teaspoon of contact lens solution. You may have to use your hands.

**STEP 4** When your slime is a stretchy, rubbery consistency, put it in a box with a lid and leave it overnight or until the bubbles disappear and the slime goes clear.

# NON-NEWTONIAN FLUIDS
# (OR WHY IS SLIME SLIMEY?)

Is slime a solid or a liquid? In some ways, it behaves like a liquid. It flows to fill the available space, just like when you pour water into different containers. But it also bounces like a solid. The answer is that slime is a non-Newtonian fluid.

The strange qualities of slime and other non-Newtonian fluids are all to do with their viscosity. This means how fast or slowly they flow. Some liquids are very viscous, meaning they flow slowly, such as honey or treacle. Other liquids aren't viscous at all and flow quickly, like water or vegetable oil. Normal (Newtonian) fluids and liquids don't change how viscous they are unless you heat them up or cool them down.

Slime is different. You can change how viscous slime is by the amount of force you use with it. The harder and more quickly you squeeze it, pull it or twist it, the more viscous it becomes. In fact, it can be so viscous that it behaves like a solid.

Try pulling the slime apart as quickly as you can.

Then try pulling it very slowly. The slime should slowly stretch and ooze apart. You may even be able to stretch it so thinly that you can see through it.

# GUMMY GOO

Finally, a slime that tastes as good as it looks. Several gummy bears will have to be sacrificed to make this slime, but it's all for the greater goo.

 **WARNING**
Ask an adult to help with handling hot sugar as it can quickly become hot enough to burn you.

 **STEP 1**
Ask an adult to melt the gummy bears in the microwave. It should take about 10–20 seconds. Be careful, the sugar can get very hot very fast.

**STEP 2**
Mix the cornflour and icing sugar together, then add it bit by bit into the melted gummy goo.

**STEP 3**
When it's cool enough to handle, use your hands to knead in the cornflour and icing sugar mix. The more you add, the less sticky the slime will be, but if you add too much, the slime will stop being stretchy. Keep going until you're at a consistency you like.

STEP 4

Add a teaspoon of vegetable oil to give the slime extra stretch.

# SLIME OLYMPICS

Now fight! Test all the different slimes to compare their properties. Make sure you have a ruler and a stopwatch to hand so you can measure the winner of each event.

Set up a ramp and see which slime is ooziest by timing how long they take to run down the ramp.

Take lumps of the different slimes that all weigh the same and see which ones stretch the furthest.

Which slime bounces the highest when you drop it? How can you measure this?